Journey
to the Heart

Centering Prayer for Children

Frank X. Jelenek
Illustrated by Ann Boyajian

PARACLETE PRESS
BREWSTER , MASSACHUSETTS

Journey to the Heart: Centering Prayer for Children

2007 First Printing
2008 Second Printing

Text copyright © 2007 by Frank X. Jelenek
Illustrations copyright © 2007 by Ann Boyajian

ISBN: 978-1-55725-482-5

Library of Congress Cataloging-in-Publication Data

Jelenek, Frank X.
 Journey to the heart : centering prayer for children / Frank X. Jelenek ;
illustrated by Ann Boyajian.
     p. cm.
 ISBN 978-1-55725-482-5
 1. Prayer–Christianity–Juvenile literature. I. Boyajian, Ann. II. Title.
BV212.J45 2007
 248.3'2–dc22   2007017666

10 9 8 7 6 5 4 3 2

Published by Paraclete Press
Brewster, Massachusetts
www.paracletepress.com

Printed in Malaysia

We are off to take a journey
to the center of ourselves.
"Where are we going?
Is it far?"

Here!
It's right here,
in the deepest part
of your heart.

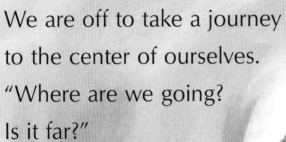

In every heart there is God's kingdom.
Your soul is the home of God inside you,
a holy place to pray each and every day.

And though you cannot see your soul,
you know it's there, just like the air.
So when you close your eyes and open
your heart, you need not go very far.
Your soul is who you are.

"Yes! Who I am is a child of God.
I am made in God's image and I'm like Jesus,
too, and a part of me is filled with the
Holy Spirit. It's true!"

Why would you want to go there, to the
deepest part of your heart? Because this
journey is a very special time when God
prays within you, in that secret place in the
soul where Jesus lives and loves.

"So, now, how do I get to that place
in my heart? Is it a long journey?
When can we start?"

No, it won't take you long—only a few
minutes, really.

But first, you will need a special, secret,
sacred word. A holy word that is a key. A
secret way to knock, a sacred key to unlock,
the center of your heart.

You can choose your own word—a secret
just between God and you.

Here are some special words to pick and
choose from:

CREATOR

faith

FATHER

HOPE

Savior

Jesus

HEAVEN

GOD

Holy Spirit

love

9

You may find another word in your Bible.
But remember, keep it safe and secret in
your heart and mind, even though you may
change it from time to time. Your key will
always work, will open every lock and door,
when it is spoken from the heart—
we know that for sure.

Do you have it—your word, I mean?
Okay, now repeat your secret word,
like a whisper in the heart, and only by God
is it heard.

Next, let me tell you the steps to take on this short journey inside. The steps are the same for everyone. Let us pray, let us rest within, with God the Father and the Son. In a very special way, silently we say, "Welcome, Holy Spirit, pray with us and in us today."

Step 1
Choose your secret-sacred word.

Step 2
Place your chairs in a circle if others join you to pray. If you're praying all by yourself, that's okay. Parents or adults may light a candle, just for as long as they stay.

Step 3

Be still. Be silent. Eyes closed.

Closed door. Feet on the floor.

Lips sealed. Straight on the seat.

Step 4

Silently say your secret word in your heart.

Rest within.

Sit and wait.

God is there inside you, in the quiet. Rest within.

Step 5

When you find yourself thinking of something else, that's okay. Just say the secret word again, silently and slowly in your heart.
Then . . .

Let those other thoughts float right out of your head.

Step 6

Six minutes of silence. A journey to the center of you with God. That is the time the journey will take you.

Step 7

Six minutes later you may open your eyes, and say out loud the "Our Father" prayer.

Do you know it?

Our Father, who art in heaven,
hallowed be thy name.
Thy kingdom come.
Thy will be done
on earth as it is in heaven.
Give us this day our daily bread,
and forgive us our trespasses
as we forgive those
who trespass against us,
and lead us not into temptation,
but deliver us from evil.

Amen.

In your heart and soul God speaks in silence, where words cannot be found, out loud. But know and trust that God will hear you, even when you don't speak a word. His ear is right next to your heart.

There may be a lot of noise outside.
A barking dog, a singing bird, a buzzing bee, a croaking frog.

Your friends might sneeze,
or cough, hiccup, maybe
even burp!

You may hear fire engines,
police sirens, airplanes and
helicopters, playtime,
laughing, yelling, and cheering.

There are also "noises" inside of you.

The thoughts of toys, TV shows, and movies.

Games and sports to play with friends and family.

Chocolate cake, ice cream, candy,

and other good things.

It's all right, they're all okay. No matter what or who you hear or think about, inside and out, just repeat your word gently, softly, quietly after each thought. It will be heard, in your heart, by God.

Let your thoughts go. Forget them all.
Let them float right out of your head.

"Knock, knock, knock! Secret, sacred Word!
Here I am, God. I want to spend time with You.
Come pray
within my heart."

God whispers back—in your heart—

I LOVE YOU!

When can you pray?

Every day that the sun rises, shines,
and sets. When stars sparkle and
twinkle, and the moon glows.

You can pray in spring, summer, fall,
and winter, as the seasons come and go.

Wake up, my child. Time to begin a new day.
Please wash, dress, have some breakfast.
Then time to pray. Six minutes of silence,
in quiet sitting, opening your heart to God today.

Then when the day is almost over, some time
before you go to bed, pray once more, to make
it twice. Six minutes more, this time of prayer
before you sleep.

Rest within your heart and soul with God,
your friend, who loves you.